Grandpa, tell us your story!

For beloved grandpa, from:

Contents

My Grandpa .... Page 3
Our most beautiful photo .... Page 4
Your family tree .... Page 5
Your parents and grandparents .... Page 6
Your childhood .... Page 11
Your adult life .... Page 17
Your life as a Dad .... Page 25
Your life as a Grandfather .... Page 33
Your whole life .... Page 39
We also wanted to know .... Page 55
Your life in pictures .... Page 59

My Grandpa

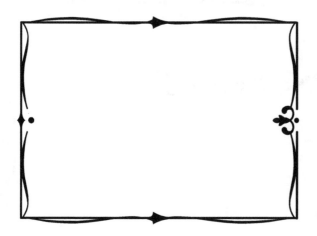

My Grandpa was born on .... in ....

His name is ....

He has .... children, ... grandchildren and .... great-grandchildren.

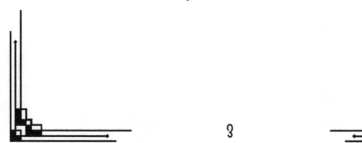
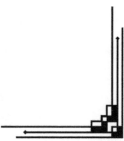

Our most beautiful photo

Your family tree

Your parents and grandparents

Tell me about your parents: what were their names? What did they do for a living? What were they like?

Your mummy:

....
....
....
....
....
....
....
....
....
....
....
....
....
....
....

Your daddy:

Where was your first home? What was it like? And your bedroom?

Did you ever go on holiday?

Do you have a picture of your parents?

And your grandparents, did you know them? Tell me a little about them too. What is your best memory with them?

Your childhood

What was your school like?

....
....
....
....
....
....
....
....

Did you work well?

....
....
....
....
....
....

What were the names of your teachers? Who did you like best? Why did you prefer them?

Were there any subjects that have disappeared today?

What were the names of your school friends? Who was your best friend?

- ....
- ....
- ....
- ....
- ....

- ....
- ....
- ....
- ....
- ....

During recess, what games did you play?

When you were doing bad things, if you ever did bad things, what were the punishments?

How did you go to school? On foot, by bike, by car ...

When you were little, what did you want to do as a grown-up?

What were your favourite games and toys?

- ....
- ....
- ....

- ....
- ....
- ....

You were a child rather ...

What is your favourite childhood memory?

A picture of you as a child

Your adult life

What was your first job? What did you do there? Did you like it?

....
....
....
....
....
....
....
....

Have you had any other experiences?

....
....
....
....
....

What were your hobbies? What did you like to do?

....
....
....
....
....
....
....
....
....
....

A picture of you having fun

Have you travelled? Where have you been?

Which moments in history have affected you the most?

Tell me about how you met Grandma:

Tell me about her ... love

How did you propose to Grandma?

Describe your wedding to me:

Did you go on a honeymoon?

When did you decide to have children?

What is your fondest memory with Grandma?

What was your biggest fight?

Attach some pictures of you here

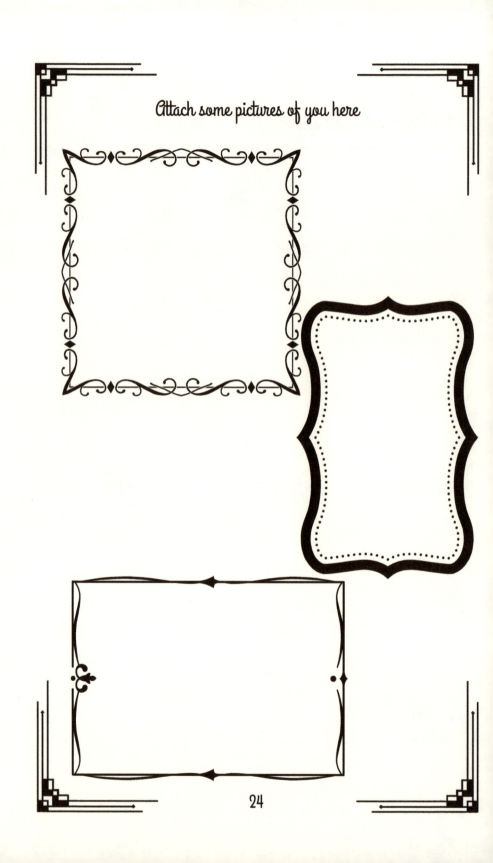

Your life as a Dad

How did you react when you found out Grandma was pregnant? How did she tell you?

How was (were) Grandma's delivery(s)? Were you with Grandma?

Did you have a lot of time to take care of your child(ren)?

And Grandma, how did he take care of them?

What did you like to do with your child(ren)?

How many children did you want? Why did you want them?

How did you choose the first name(s)?

Which ones did you prefer?

- ....
- ....
- ....
- ....
- ....
- ....

- ....
- ....
- ....
- ....
- ....
- ....

What was the biggest mischief made by your child(ren)?

What was your reaction? What about Granny's?

What did you like most about being a daddy? ☺

And what did you find most distressing?

Attach some photos of your family here

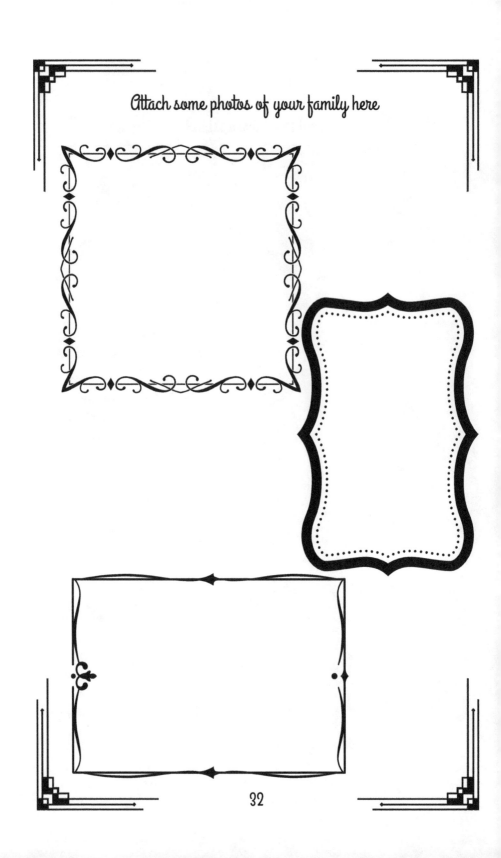

Your life as a Grandfather

At what age did you become a Grandfather?

....
....
....
....
....
....

How did you feel?

....
....
....
....
....
....
....
....
....
....

What do you play with your grandchild(ren)?
Do you play the same games as with your child(ren)?

What do you prefer to do when you are with your grandchild(ren)?

Mum says you don't listen to her when she asks you not to give away too many cakes and candies ...
Is that true?

Sometimes I hear you say that your grandchild(ren) tires you .... Is this true?

When you were little, did you do the same silly things as your grandchild(ren)?

How much do you love your grandchild(ren)?

Are there things that your grandchild(ren) can do that you used to say no to your child(ren) about?

What is your best memory with your grandchild(ren)?

Your most beautiful memories in photos

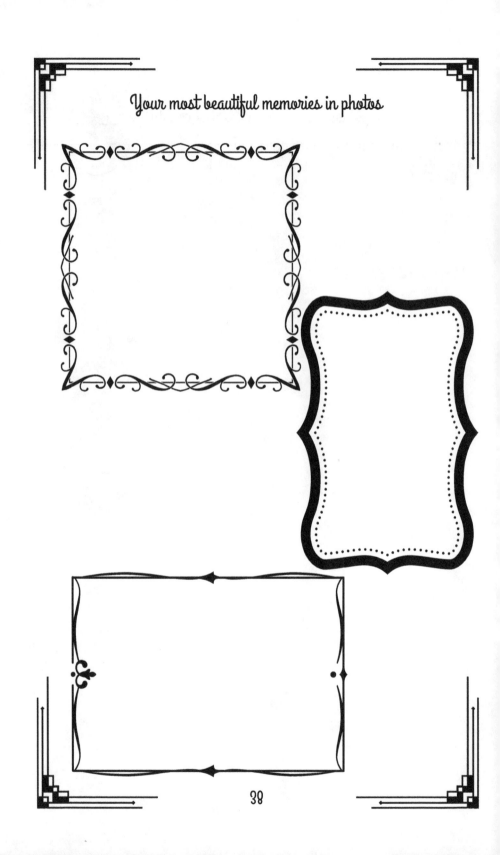

Your whole life

What are your most beautiful moments?
And the most difficult ones?

Did you realise your dreams? Which ones?

dream

What do you love most in your life?

What are your greatest fears?

What are your pleasures today?

Do you think your life is full? What are you most proud of?

Are there other things you would like to do?

What advice can you give your grandchild(ren) to be happy?

What advice can you give your grandchild(ren) to be happy and to grow in their professional life?

We also wanted to know...
(Additional questions to be written by children and grandchildren)

Your life in pictures

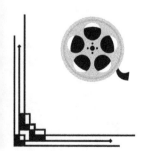

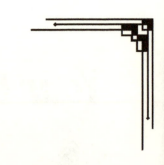

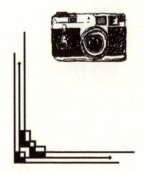
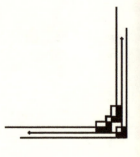

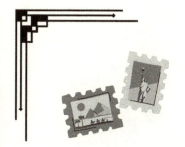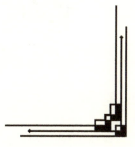

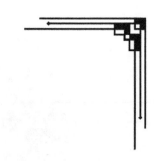

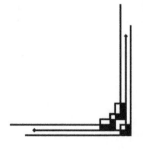

www.ingramcontent.com/pod-product-compliance
Lightning Source LLC
LaVergne TN
LVHW040924221224
799711LV00026B/208